Exploring Friendships,
Puberty and Relationships

of related interest

Making Sense of Sex
A Forthright Guide to Puberty, Sex and Relationships for People with Asperger's Syndrome
Sarah Attwood
Illustrated by Jonathon Powell
ISBN 978 1 84310 374 5
eISBN 978 1 84642 797 8

Sexuality and Relationship Education for Children and Adolescents with Autism Spectrum Disorders
A Professional's Guide to Understanding, Preventing Issues, Supporting Sexuality and Responding to Inappropriate Behaviours
Davida Hartman
Illustrated by Kate Brangan
ISBN 978 1 84905 385 3
eISBN 978 0 85700 755 1

The Social and Life Skills MeNu
A Skill Building Workbook for Adolescents with Autism Spectrum Disorders
Karra M. Barber
ISBN 978 1 84905 861 2
eISBN 978 0 85700 433 8

Exploring **Friendships**, **Puberty** and **Relationships**

A Programme to Help Children and Young People on the Autism Spectrum to Cope with the Challenges of Adolescence

Kate Ripley

Jessica Kingsley *Publishers*
London and Philadelphia

First published in 2014
by Jessica Kingsley Publishers
73 Collier Street
London N1 9BE, UK
and
400 Market Street, Suite 400
Philadelphia, PA 19106, USA

www.jkp.com

Copyright © Kate Ripley 2014

Front cover image source: Shutterstock®. The cover image is for illustrative purposes only, and any person featuring is a model.

All rights reserved. No part of this publication may be reproduced in any material form (including photocopying of any pages other than those marked with a ✓, storing it in any medium by electronic means and whether or not transiently or incidentally to some other use of this publication) without the written permission of the copyright owner except in accordance with the provisions of the Copyright, Designs and Patents Act 1988 or under the terms of a licence issued by the Copyright Licensing Agency Ltd, Saffron House, 6–10 Kirby Street, London EC1N 8TS. Applications for the copyright owner's written permission to reproduce any part of this publication should be addressed to the publisher.

Warning: The doing of an unauthorised act in relation to a copyright work may result in both a civil claim for damages and criminal prosecution.

All pages marked ✓ may be photocopied for personal use with this programme, but may not be reproduced for any other purposes without the permission of the publisher.

Library of Congress Cataloging in Publication Data
A CIP catalog record for this book is available from the Library of Congress

British Library Cataloguing in Publication Data
A CIP catalogue record for this book is available from the British Library

ISBN 978 1 84905 439 3

Printed and bound in Great Britain

Contents

Acknowledgements 7
Introduction 9

Part 1: The Challenges of Early Adolescence
1 This Is Me 20
2 Me and My World 25
3 Friendships 27
4 My Network 29
5 Who Do I Trust? 31
6 Making Friends 33
7 Making Friends Online 35
8 Gender Identity 38
9 We Are All Different 41
10 We All Grow Up and Change 43
11 Look into the Future 46

Part 2: Puberty and Preparation for Adult Relationships
12 Understanding our Bodies 50
13 Personal Hygiene 53
14 Things People Worry About Around Puberty 58
15 Expectations About How We Behave 62
16 Behaviour in Public Space and Private Space 66
17 Expectations Change 68
18 What the Law Says 73
19 Making Friends 76
20 Being a Friend 79
21 From Friendships to Relationships 81
22 Things Are Not Always What They Seem 83
23 Thinking About a Relationship 85

24	Eat Well and Be Healthy	88
25	A Balanced Diet	90
26	Getting to Know You	92
27	Reading the Hidden Messages	97
28	It Takes Two: Dealing with Setbacks	100
29	Building a Relationship	102
30	Safe Sex	105

Appendix 1: Tutor Notes	111
Appendix 2: Baseline Assessments	114
References	119

Strength Cards	121
Friendship Cards	125
Situation Cards	129
About Me Cards	131
Personal Space Cards	137
Actions Cards	139
Response Cards	141
Public Space or Private Space Cards	143
Clothing Cards	145

Acknowledgements

Nicole Lowe, manager of the resourced provision of Robert May's School, Odiham, and Julie Chapman, support assistant, who delivered the programme during the academic years 2011–2013. They have provided valuable feedback about the sessions and this has been used to guide the revisions of the programme. Together with the students they have contributed exciting additional ideas.

The students in the Resourced Provision at Robert May's School who participated in the sessions. They professed to enjoy them and took their role as constructive critics very seriously.

Jamie Coe who carried out baseline assessments of the understanding that students had about relationships, gender and personal identity as part of her doctoral training.

Diane Sambrook for her preparation of drafts of the manuscript.

Hampshire Local Authority for supporting the development of the programme.

Introduction

The pathway through adolescence is a challenge for everyone. For young people with autism spectrum disorders (ASDs) who experience difficulties with social communication and the development and maintenance of friendships, the adolescent years may be particularly challenging and confusing (Lawson, 2005). Young people have sexual feelings and, although people with ASDs experience physical and sexual development at a similar age to their peers, emotionally they are likely to function at a much younger level (Sicile-Kira, 2006). They may also have more limited opportunities to learn about sexuality due to fewer social contacts through friendship groups (Stokes, Newton and Kaur, 2007). For many young people, informal knowledge of sexual matters comes through interactions and observations of others (Koller, 2000) but Stokes *et al.* found that unlike their neurotypical peers, young people on the autism spectrum were not learning romantic skills from parents, observations or the media.

The majority of teenagers receive information about puberty and sex from a range of sources that may not be so accessible to an individual on the autism spectrum. They discuss personal or vicarious experiences with their peers and learn from watching the behaviour of others. Adolescents on the autism spectrum have fewer opportunities to learn about and discuss sexual exploration experiences with friends and are more likely to get information from the media. However, they may not understand the emotional and social context of what they see in films and television 'soaps' or read in magazines and newspapers. As for most adolescents, there are also opportunities to visit explicit sites on the internet. Boys may start looking at pornographic sites from the age of 11 according to the findings of the Sex Education Forum 2003 (National Children's Bureau, 2003). Information about girls accessing pornographic sites has not yet been the focus of research.

A further issue for young people on the autism spectrum is that of gender identity. Limited social awareness and a reduced drive to conform to gender-related norms may influence how they are perceived by peers and lead to negative labelling.

Clinical experience of working with three Resourced Provisions[1] for students with high-functioning ASDs/Asperger's syndrome in mainstream schools has, over time, raised issues around sexual identity for a significant number of adolescent boys. Several of them had queried openly whether they might be homosexual although none of them reported feelings of sexual attraction towards other boys. Their confusion about personal identity focused upon their:

- preferred activities and interests that were different from most of their male peers
- choices of companions so that they felt more comfortable interacting with girls and often perceived male peers as bullying them
- behaviours such as inappropriate touching of boys and girls, which triggered negative labelling by peers.

---

1   A Resourced Provision is a facility attached to a mainstream primary or secondary school that supports the needs of children who have special needs: in this case, the needs of students with autism.

Concerns about how best to support these adolescents provided the initial impetus for the development of this programme. Subsequent developments of the programme have extended the materials to include the needs of adolescent girls as well as boys.

The development of a gender identity follows a clear sequence in neurotypical individuals (Slaby and Frey, 1975):

- identification: labelling of one's own sex and that of others
- the concept of stability: gender remains the same over time
- the concept of consistency: gender remains fixed and is not altered by superficial transformations such as a change of clothing.

Kohlberg (1966) argues that the achievement of gender consistency motivates children to attend to gender norms and to learn gender concepts and the behaviours to which they attempt to conform. As part of this process, children will start to pay selective attention to same sex role models (Slaby and Frey, 1975). They will start to engage in same sex activities, so that boys who conform to a male role model will for example choose to play football on the playground, while girls will play with dolls (Warin, 2000). Clothing may be chosen according to gender, often encouraged by the adults around them who may buy pretty dresses or even bra-tops for pre-pubescent girls. Exposure to the media may reinforce the idea of gender stereotypes so that by 5–6 years of age children show evaluated reactions to males and females (de Lisi and Johns, 1984) and respond to gender cues (Zucker and Bradley, 2000).

As neurotypical children develop their understanding of gender stability and consistency, the gender stereotypes that are held quite rigidly at about five years begin to show more flexibility (Signorella, Bigler and Liben, 1993). The development of these quite abstract concepts is linked more to the social emotional stage of development of an individual than to their chronological age and physical maturity (Tissot, 2009). Young people on the autism spectrum who have inherent difficulties with social awareness are therefore at risk of delays and confusion in the area of gender identity.

There is some evidence that adolescents on the autism spectrum experience more confusion about gender identity than their neurotypical peers. This evidence comes from the disproportionate incidence of referral to clinics for gender identity disorders (GID) of people on the autism spectrum. In a study that came out in 2010, de Vries *et al.* found that young people with autism who were referred to GID clinics were mostly attracted to the opposite sex rather than to the same sex and, therefore, did not meet the criteria (Diagnostic and Statistical Manual of Mental Disorders, Fourth Edition: DSM-IV) for a gender identity disorder. These young people questioned their sexual identity for several reasons that were linked to their autism rather than to other factors. These included:

- they reported feelings of being different from their peers in childhood and they attributed this to gender dysmorphia (de Vries *et al.*, 2010)
- boys showed 'feminine' interests in soft materials, hair and so on that could be attributed to preferences for sensory input (de Vries *et al.*, 2010), and avoided 'rough' play (Mukaddes, 2002)
- rigid gender beliefs were more like the concepts found in younger children and more concordant with emotional age than chronological age (de Vries *et al.*, 2010)

- they might show fetish type behaviour associated with particular interests, for example wellington boots (de Vries *et al.*, 2010)
- they do not respond like neurotypicals to the strong role pressures and concerns about the violation of the norms for gender linked behaviour that contribute to group identity and inclusion.

There has been less research with reference to girls on the autism spectrum partly because boys have been, historically, easier to diagnose. However, girls on the autism spectrum may often relate better with boys because of similar linear conversation and thinking. Baron-Cohen (2002) might describe them as systematisers like neurotypical boys, and career choices may follow what society sees as typically male, such as engineering, ICT or accounting. Gomez de la Cuesta and Mason (2010) describe a double glass ceiling because of society's expectation of girls and women regarding looks, clothing, presentation of self, social skills, empathy and dating. These expectations assume more significance as girls enter the secondary phase of their education.

Many students on the autism spectrum experience a heightened awareness of the issues around personal, gender and sexual identity when they make the transition to secondary school. The awareness and potential confusions that they experience are compounded by the physical changes associated with puberty and the different expectations for behaviour that attend a more adult physical appearance. This programme has been designed to address these significant areas of difficulty for adolescents on the autism spectrum.

The *Exploring Friendships, Puberty and Relationships* programme described in this book has been developed to support young people on the autism spectrum to understand more about gender identity and puberty and to navigate the shoals of making and breaking relationships. They typically have a limited background experience of friendships and so the potential for confusion and frustration is that much more acute.

The development of the programme

The original impetus for this programme came from clinical experience of working with adolescents on the autism spectrum. As a starting point for the development of the programme the concerns that were expressed by teaching staff and the knowledge and understanding of the students themselves were explored.

The experiences of staff in mainstream secondary schools were elicited by means of structured interviews (Coe, 2011). Thematic analysis of the transcripts identified seven core themes:

1. differences in the behaviour of the students as they approached puberty, some of which were related directly to sexuality and others to changes in attitudes to school work
2. anxiety from staff about addressing sexuality and gender issues in school and concern about the boundaries for their involvement
3. some practical strategies that staff had tried which included talking to the students and their parents but a general concern about their level of knowledge and 'expertise' to provide support
4. a need for resources to help staff to work with the students effectively and with more confidence

5. confusion among the students themselves, about what might be 'normal' in terms of sexual development and feelings: their limited understanding of what constitutes appropriate behaviour particularly around touching and talking about sexual matters

6. a tendency towards making interpretations about the gender or sexuality of other students based on observable, yet superficial differences in behaviour or dress code

7. concern that the students had a limited understanding despite having attended the school-based UK PHSE (personal, health, social education) programmes: teachers referred specifically to difficulties with expressing feelings, accepting difference in others and a reluctance to talk about these issues that they found confusing and threatening: '…don't like dealing with sex and everything that has to do with it.'

The *Exploring Friendships, Puberty and Relationships* programme was planned to address the issues that had been raised by the staff who were interviewed.

The second source of information that was used to plan the programme content came from the students themselves. Four baseline assessments were carried out with students who attended a resourced provision for high functioning autism in a mainstream secondary school (see Appendix 2). During and following the assessments the students were reassured that the answers they gave would remain confidential and that it was not a test for which they would receive marks. It was explained that the activities were to help the team to understand their views and feelings.

Three baseline assessments were completed independently:

1. the Growing Up questionnaire: ten items with a five-point Likert response scale
2. definitions and colloquialisms for ten sexual terms or phrases
3. gender stereotypes (based on a framework by Ruble *et al.*, 2007): Who does what? Boys/men or girls/women?

The fourth assessment involved an exploration of the personal constructs of each student. Personal construction analysis explores how people understand themselves and their world (Ravenette, 1999).

The programme was written to reflect the concerns of adults who work with adolescents on the autism spectrum together with the knowledge and understanding of the students themselves. A pilot version of the programme was introduced to students in 2011 and the programme evolved with the help of feedback from both the students and the facilitators of the programme.

About the programme

Part 1 of the programme introduces the idea of gender identity and builds upon the skills of social communication, social understanding and friendships that are addressed in existing programmes. There is a focus on personal identity and how people grow and change.

Part 2 of the programme addresses issues around puberty and the more complex rules around relationships and behaviour that are associated with the move from childhood through adolescence to adult life. For neurotypical adolescents the skills that are involved build upon existing experiences of friendship and managing relationships needed with their peers. Adolescents on the autism spectrum may have practised the skills in the structure of a social skills group but may not have achieved a fluency level to be comfortable in the school or local community. Their limited social understanding may lead to confusion about various conventions such as:

- behaviour in public/private settings
- conventions about touching
- consent
- dress codes
- self-care and hygiene
- desired and non-desired contact which can lead to police involvement, such as for stalking.

Part 1 of the programme has been trialled with students aged 11–13 years and Part 2 with older students. However, the age ranges should be considered to be flexible according to the needs of individual students and groups of students.

For many existing social skills programmes there is limited research evidence about their efficacy. School staff will often say that students have attended social skills groups over a number of years but there has been no discernible, or measured, change in their functional behaviour outside the structure of the group.

The *Exploring Friendships, Puberty and Relationships* programme follows three principles that have been shown to contribute to positive, effective outcomes for the students:

1. The sessions focus on skills that the members of the group need to learn, based on a careful analysis of their existing skills.
2. The sessions are well structured and planned as rigorously as any other lesson.
3. The skills that are addressed in the sessions are practised in the context of the home and school environment through the 'missions' that are set as challenges following each meeting of the group. Role models are their neurotypical peers and the skills are generalised outside the structure of the group. At the start of each session the participants give feedback about the outcome of their 'mission' to the group.

The students who have experienced the programme have shown positive gains in terms of their confidence in social situations and their ability to manage social challenges. The students and the adult facilitators have also reported that they have enjoyed the sessions. Having fun together has helped to build relationships and keep the students fully engaged.

How to use the programme

The programme consists of 30 session plans. As noted above, the themes in Part 1 have mainly been used with students aged 11–13 and the themes in Part 2 with older students. However, these age ranges are only guidelines. The sessions do follow a progression and so it is intended that they should be delivered in sequential order. However, some students may be ready to access Part 2 at a younger age while other students may be older when they are ready to move on to Part 2.

The session plans provide a framework for discussion around a theme which is identified by the heading. *The session plans are not intended to be used as worksheets for the students.* There are some resources that can be photocopied for students to use and these are indicated in the programme with a ✓. The sessions are planned around a theme and in practice the facilitators have found that some sessions can extend over two or even three meetings of the group. For example, Theme 13, 'Personal Hygiene', extended over three meetings of the pilot group.

It is recommended that the sessions are facilitated by two adults, with one acting as a process facilitator and the other with the role of supporting individual students and observing engagement/participation. After each session the facilitators discuss the activities for relevance, accessibility and enjoyment. Any changes to the materials or session plan are recorded for future reference. Typically, sessions are planned for 40–45 minutes, the duration of a lesson in a typical secondary school.

Planning practicalities for the group will include:

- *the timing of the sessions:* it is desirable for sessions to take place at the same time each week but subject teachers and students may not like to miss the same lesson each week
- *venue:* a space which is quiet with minimal interruptions anticipated and not a classroom where different expectations for interaction styles pre-exist
- consideration of whether *refreshments* should be available
- *selection* of participants.

The students in the groups should be selected because they need to learn and practise the skills that are addressed in the programme. Baseline assessment of the skills and understanding of the students on the long-list for the group is recommended to ensure homogeneity of the group. Examples of baseline assessments you can use are included in Appendix 2.

A group of six students is an optimal number for high-functioning adolescents on the autism spectrum, but smaller numbers may be more appropriate for students who have more significant difficulties. For some students supplementary individual work may be appropriate, for example around issues of masturbation or personal hygiene. Students in the groups can be drawn from different age cohorts as the groups are convened according to need, social and emotional age, rather than chronological age.

Each meeting has a consistent plan so that the students are aware of the structure. This helps to ensure that levels of anxiety about changes of routine are minimised. A typical meeting plan might include:

- a warm-up activity, which is the same for each session
- feedback from the previous week's mission
- introduction of the topic for the meeting
- activities that practise the new topic
- discussion of individual missions for the next week
- a closing activity, which is the same for each session.

A sample session plan for Theme 3, 'Friendships' (based on activities 3 and 4), is described in detail below. The plan illustrates the structure of a meeting as described above: practitioners will need to define the objectives for each of their sessions and how the objectives will be met (i.e. what activities they will introduce and the resources they will need).

Theme 3
Friendships

Objective
To help students identify friendship qualities in others.

Resources
    Flip chart and pens
    Friendship Cards
    Large cards made up by facilitator | Friend | | ? | (don't know) | Not friend |
    Copy of Mission: 'What I value in a friend…'
    Strength Cards

Warm-up activity
- *Something good:* students take turns to say something good that happened since the last meeting

and/or

- *Empty chair:* students take turns to invite someone to sit in the empty chair to their right

or

- Any other warm-up activity that the facilitators like to use.

Feedback from the previous theme's mission
Tell me one thing that you learned from talking about your family tree with your family.

Share the family tree and any pictures with the group.

Topic for the meeting
Friends

Activities
1. Students write down the names of their friends.
2. Students choose one friend.

3. Students sort the Friendship Cards into the categories ⬚Friend⬚ ⬚?⬚ ⬚Not friend⬚ as a group activity with discussion.
4. Students use the Friendship Cards to describe 'my friend'.
5. Students discuss what qualities they would not choose in a friend using the Friendship Cards as a prompt. Use the flip chart to record ideas.

Mission

Think about what you value in a friend.

Write down some ideas on the Mission sheet and bring them to the next session.

Closing activity

Choose a Strength Card to give to another person in the group.

At later meetings add: 'I have chosen this card for (name) because…'

Facilitators may prefer their own choice of activity or a relaxation exercise.

The sensitivity of some of the topics under discussion should be acknowledged and students are encouraged to post any questions that they have in a Questions Box which is available between the meetings. The facilitators can decide when they read a question whether it would be suitable for discussion with the whole group (the questioner remaining anonymous) or whether it should be addressed with that student individually. If the facilitators are of the same gender (female in the case of the pilot study), it may be helpful for the students to know that a different (male) member of staff is available to talk to them as an option.

The parents of students on the autism spectrum may have a resurgence of anxiety around the transition to secondary school about how their child will manage the social demands of relationships as they get older and achieve independence and loving partnerships. Sexuality is often a particular concern for parents, (Ruble and Dalrymple, 1993) and represents a challenge for many adults who are sensitive about discussing the topic per se, but particularly when it is linked to any form of disability. It is, therefore, recommended practice to discuss the programme with the parents/carers of the participants and elicit their support for the missions – generalisation exercises that are carried out at home and at school. The senior management team may also suggest that the introduction of the programme is discussed with school governors.

Strength Cards

Adolescents on the autism spectrum frequently have low self-esteem, and find it hard to acknowledge their strengths and to accept praise. The Strength Cards can be used to end any session on a positive note, as illustrated in the sample session plan on the preceding page.

There are 38 cards available so it helps to select some cards each time that are relevant to the group or the topic that has been the focus of the session. The selected cards are placed face up, on the floor or a table for the students to choose a card.

The cards may be used in a flexible way that responds to the growing confidence and social skills of the students.

1. Students choose a card for themselves, read out the message, thus taking ownership of the positive statement. The card is then returned to the array so that other students may select the same card, if they wish to do so.

    When the students are comfortable with this exercise some alternatives that are more socially demanding can be introduced.

2. Students choose a card for another member of the group using free choice, or can be directed to make a structured choice of the person to their left or right in the circle.

    This exercise may be made more demanding following discussion about how to respond to a compliment. Thus, with practice, the students build up to the donor looking at the receiver and smiling when presenting the card, and the receiver looking at the donor, and smiling and saying 'thank you'.

3. Students choose a card for themselves but say why they have chosen that card, for example what they did to be helpful.

4. Students choose a card for another group member and say why they have chosen that card for that person.

The Strength Cards can be used in other different ways and tutors might like to add new cards to meet the needs of their students.

Tutor notes

Additional instructions for tutors are included in some of the sessions. These are marked with a *. Whenever you see this symbol, refer to Appendix 1.

PART 1
The Challenges of Early Adolescence

Theme 1
This Is Me*

| Name: |
| Age: |
| Where I live: |
| Who I live with: |
| What I look like (physical appearance: height, hair and eye colour, etc.): |

1. Guess who?*

Pick up a picture from the table but don't show it to anyone else. Do you know who this person is? Describe the person to the others, but don't tell them the name of the person. Can people recognise this person from the description you give?

Copyright © Kate Ripley 2014

2. Write a physical description or draw a picture of someone that you all know. Show/read your description to the group. Can they guess who you are describing?

My mystery person:

3. My interests*
What I like to do

At home:

At school:

What I really do not like

At home:

At school:

Who else likes what I like?

Who else in your group shares your interests?

I like	Other people like
e.g. Computer games	e.g. Joe Bloggs
1.	
2.	
3.	
4.	
5.	
6.	
7.	
8.	
9.	
10.	

4. Theme 1 Mission*

Find two people in your tutor group who match with you for at least one interest.

What is it?

Find out which members of your family share at least one interest.

What is it?

Introduce the Questions Box

Ask the students to write on a card or slip of paper any questions that they are reluctant to discuss in the group.

Let the students know where the Questions Box will be kept and that it is available for posting messages at any time.

Reassure them that if they are worried about something others will be as well.

Discuss any common questions anonymously in the group. Students are given the choice of whether to sign their question or to remain anonymous. Offer individual discussions for students if they wish to talk privately about their concerns.

Let students know that the Questions Box is available between sessions. Offer individual support if appropriate.

Theme 2
Me and My World

---

1. Feedback from Theme 1 Mission

Who in your tutor group shares one of your interests?

Who in your family shares one of your interests?

---

2. Groups we are born into
Discussion

Develop a flow chart like the example below on the flip chart. Get the students to discuss 'who are my family?'

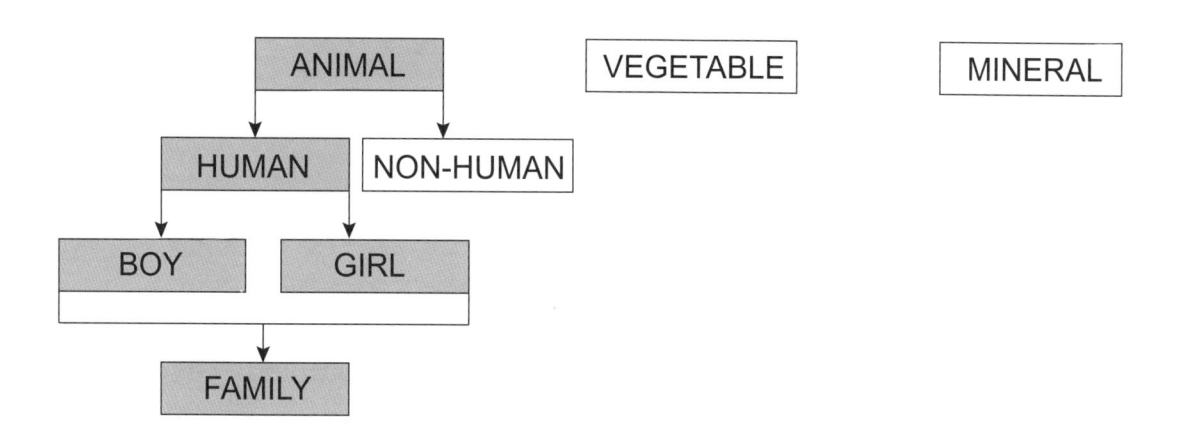

```
ANIMAL            VEGETABLE            MINERAL
  │
  ├──────────┐
  ▼          ▼
HUMAN    NON-HUMAN
  │
  ├──────────┐
  ▼          ▼
 BOY        GIRL
  │
  ▼
FAMILY
```

3. My family tree

Everyone's family tree will look different. Help the students to draw their own family tree, complete with step-parents/siblings. The example overleaf represents a conventional family tree that some students will be able to use. Build up a simple family tree with the students. Then build up one to reflect step-relationships and other varieties. Help the students to construct their own family trees on a large sheet of paper.

Family tree

Can you put names in all the spaces on your family tree?

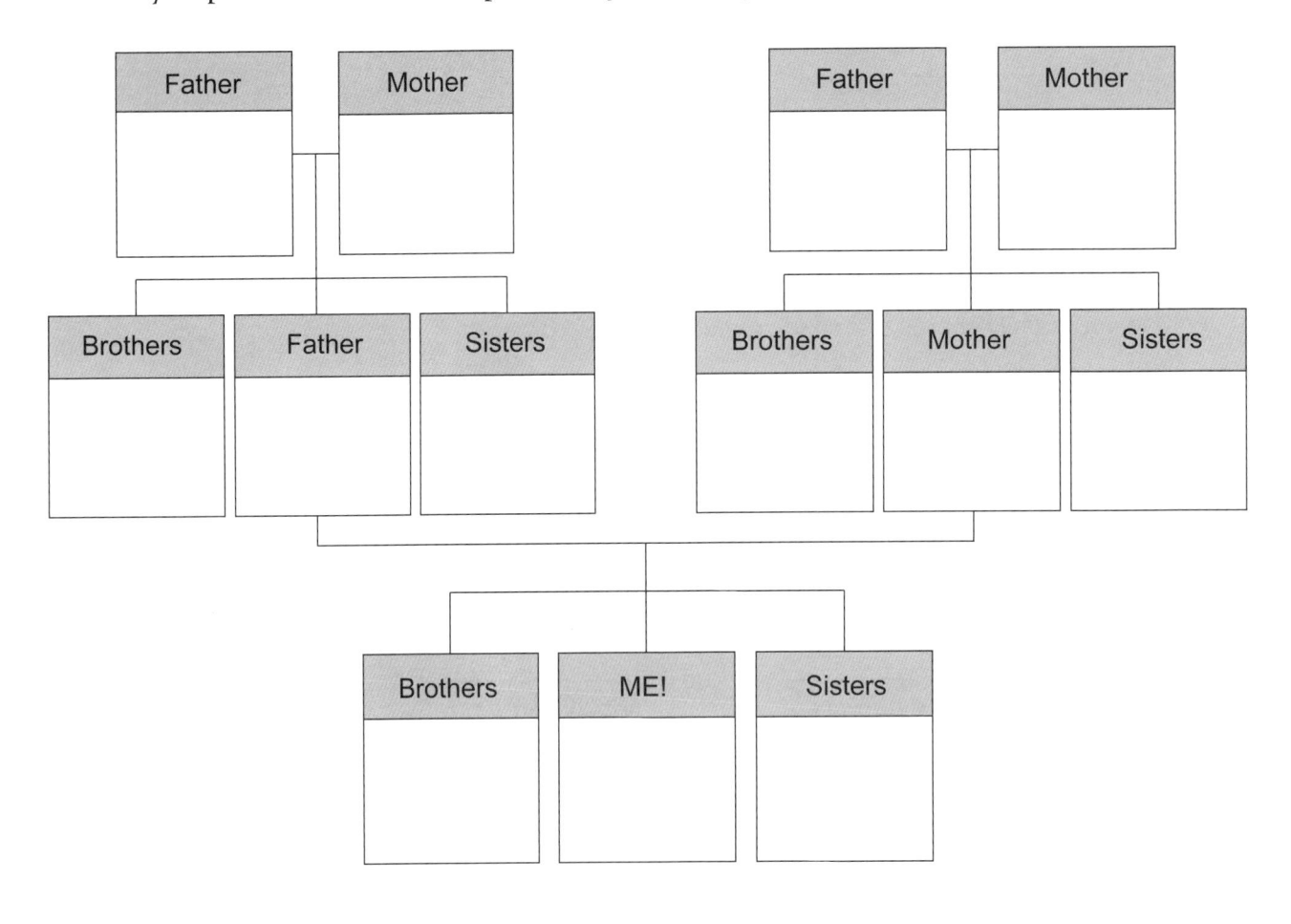

```
[Father] [Mother]                          [Father] [Mother]
    |                                          |
[Brothers] [Father] [Sisters]          [Brothers] [Mother] [Sisters]
                |                                    |
                +------------------+-----------------+
                                   |
                      [Brothers] [ME!] [Sisters]
```

---

4. Theme 2 Mission*

Talk to your family about the family tree. Can you add any more people to the tree?

If you have some pictures to share, bring them to the next session.

Theme 3
Friendships

1. Feedback from Theme 2 Mission
Share your family tree and pictures with the group.

2. Friendships

Ask students to think about the qualities their friends at school have (in both tutor groups and subject groups).

My friends are:

Choose one friend. Select the Friendship Cards that describe why they are your friend.

My friend is:

3. Card sorting activity*

Sort the Friendship Cards into the following categories: Friend | ? | Not friend

4. My friend*

Use the Friendship Cards to discuss what you would not choose in a friend. Think about someone who you would not like to have as a friend. Use the cards to help you think about what they might do.

I would not like to be a friend to someone who:

5. Theme 3 Mission

Think about what you value in a friend.

Write down some ideas and bring them to the next session.

Theme 4
My Network

1. Feedback from Theme 3 Mission
Discuss the qualities that you think are important in a friend.

2. Groups we can join

Some people belong to groups such as swimming club, scouts, a church group, etc.

Fill in the gaps in the chart to show which groups you belong to. You can use a picture or photograph instead of writing. You do not need to fill all the circles – or you may want to add some more.

3. Share your chart with the rest of the group to see what things everyone does outside school.

4. Look at all the groups that people belong to. Are there any groups or activities that you would like to join?

Copyright © Kate Ripley 2014

Groups we can join

ME

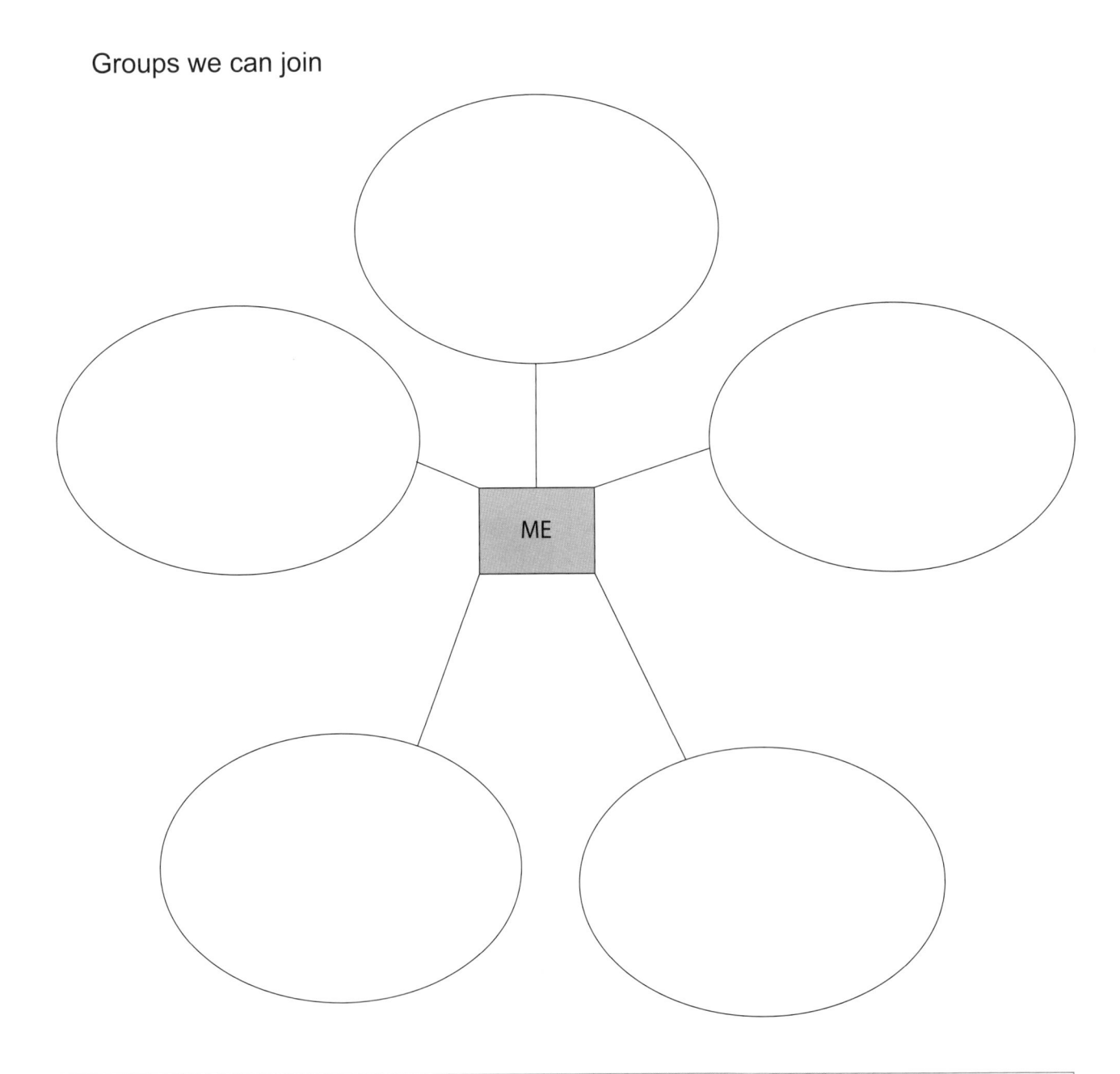

5. Theme 4 Mission

Think of one new group or activity that you would like to join.

Talk to your family about new things they could help you do.

Theme 5
Who Do I Trust?*

1. Feedback from Theme 4 Mission
What ideas did you have about new groups to join or activities to try?

2. Who would I trust?*

1. I need help with my homework.
   I would go to: _____

2. I lost my mobile phone.
   I would go to: _____

3. Someone took my bag and threw it down the stairs.
   I would go to: _____

4. I had a great time at the weekend.
   I would tell: _____

5. I did really well in the test:
   I would tell: _____

6. I feel lonely.
   I would go to: _____

7. I need to borrow money for lunch.
   I would ask: _____

8. Someone called me names and I feel upset.
   I would go to: _____

9. I have a new track on my iPod.
   I would share it with: _____

10. I am going on an exciting trip.
    I would tell: _____

Copyright © Kate Ripley 2014

3. Desert island

You are marooned on a desert island and could take one person with you.

Who would it be?

Why did you choose that person?
- Share some of your ideas.
- Who did you trust the most?

4. Make a group list on the flip chart of the people in your lives that you trust and could go to when things go wrong.

---

5. Theme 5 Mission

You have lost your maths homework book. Think about who you would go to. Practise what you would say to them.

You have forgotten your PE kit. Think about who you would go to. Practise what you would say to them.

Choose one of these examples to share with the group next time.

Theme 6
Making Friends

1. Feedback from Theme 5 Mission
Share with the group who you would go to when you have lost your homework or PE kit, and what you would say to them.

2. Circle of friends*

Think about your family, friends and people you know.

Add some names to each of the circles.

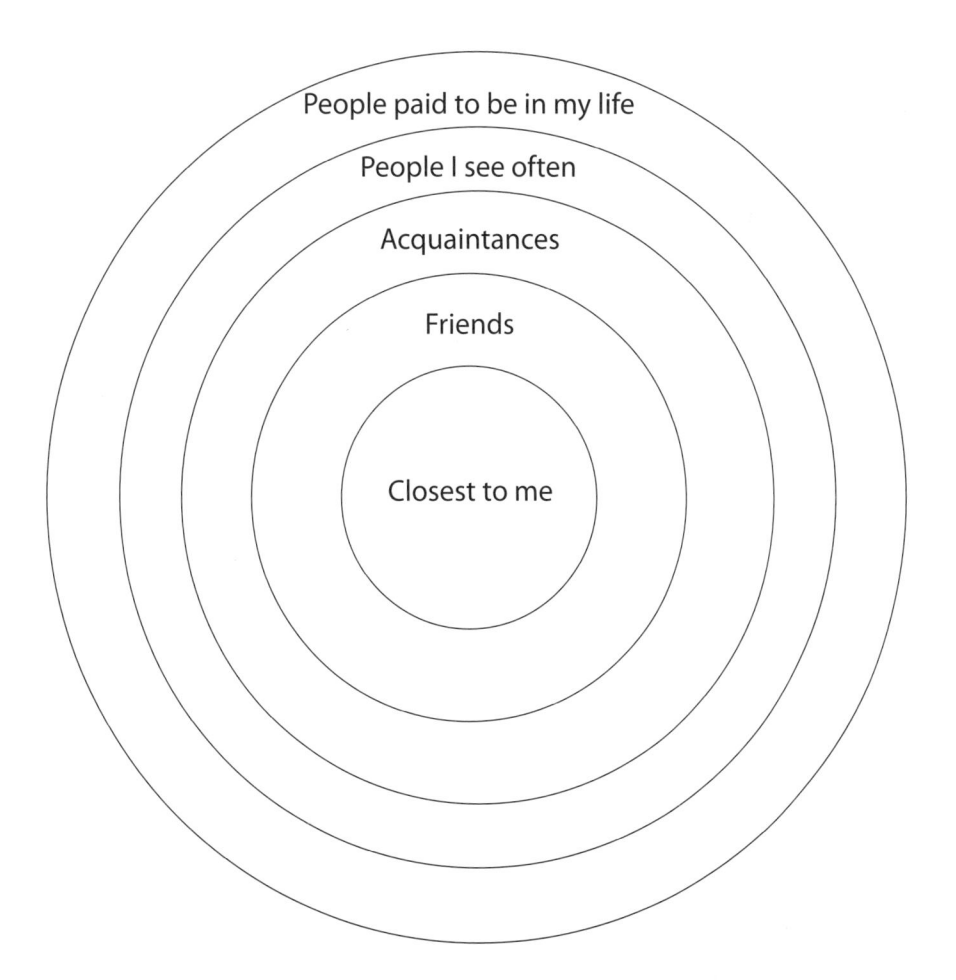

- People paid to be in my life
- People I see often
- Acquaintances
- Friends
- Closest to me

3. Discuss the chart to explore the difference between a friend, an acquaintance and someone you just see often. Is your behaviour towards them different?

Copyright © Kate Ripley 2014

4. Think about those people who you named as most trusted from Theme 5. Write their names in the table below:

Person	Where do they fit in the circle of friends?

5. Making friends

Do you remember some of the things that help us to make friends?

- Look at them and smile.
- Ask them about themselves.
- Listen to what they say and respond to that (maintain the topic).
- Take equal turns in the conversation.
- Explore things you both like/are interested in.
- When it feels safe to do so, share some personal thoughts and feelings.

6. Theme 6 Mission

Think of one person in your tutor group, class or year group that you would like to get to know.

Try to start a conversation with them.

Choose your moment.

Look at them and smile.

Ask them about something you know they like.

Can you keep the conversation going?

Theme 7
Making Friends Online

1. Feedback from Theme 6 Mission

Ask each student how their conversation developed.

Have they spoken to that person again?

2. Facebook

Ask the students if they have a Facebook account.

Does anyone in their family have an account?

Do their friends have an account?

Discuss:

- To open an account you will be asked for your:
    - name
    - email address
    - a password
    - whether you are male or female.
- Any other information is optional – you don't have to give it.
- There are other questions that you can choose to answer – for example, your school or workplace and your address. You may want to say the town where you live.
- Think carefully before you enter this information. Discuss why in the group.

3. Your online profile

Write an online profile, which might include your interests and the music or sports you like. Some of the prompts such as religion, political views or the languages you speak may be for older people. You can leave these boxes blank.

Here is an example of an online profile:

> My name is John. I am 15 years old and I live in Alton.
>
> I am looking for a friend of about the same age who likes to listen to music and play Warhammer games like me.
>
> I also like to ride my bike and add new gadgets to it.
>
> Do you like the same things?

Discuss as a group what the students might put in their online profile.

On your online account you can decide:
- who can see your stuff
- who can contact you.

You may leave your online profile open for anyone to read.

Discuss in the group whether it is OK for anyone to read the students' profiles.

4. How to be safe

- People are supposed to use their real names, ages and identities online. *But* unless you have met the person already, they may not be who they say they are.

Discuss this in the group.

- Any information that you post can be copied and distributed in ways that you did not intend.

Discuss this in the group. Examples may be comments made when angry or personal photographs.

Think before you post. You may receive messages that you don't like, for example:
- hurtful messages
- pictures that make you feel uncomfortable
- requests for pictures of you that you could not show your teachers or parents.

If this happens, IGNORE them or:
- ask the person to stop
- unfriend, or block the person
- tell your parents or teacher.

Facebook gives tips for staying safe – look online.

Tips for teens from Facebook
- Don't share your password with anyone.
- Only accept friend requests from people you know.
- Don't post anything you would not want your parents or teachers to see.
- Be honest about yourself and what you like.
- Learn about the privacy settings.

Discuss the tips with the group.

Many schools now have their own guidance about how to keep safe online. Discuss the school guidance with the group.

5. Theme 7 Mission
Write an online profile for yourself and bring it to our next session.

Theme 8
Gender Identity

1. Feedback from Theme 7 Mission
Share your online profile with the group.

> Sugar and spice and all things nice
> That's what little girls are made of
> Slugs and snails and puppy dog's tails
> That's what little boys are made of.

2. Girls and women

What do you think about them?

Write down some ideas about: appearance, what they do, wear, like, leisure activities, the sorts of people they are.

3. Using the flip chart, collate the ideas from the group which are shared by group members.

4. Boys and men

What do you think about them?

Write down some ideas about: appearance, what they do, wear, like, leisure activities, the sorts of people they are.

5. Using the flip chart, collate the ideas from the group which are shared by group members.

6. Using the flip chart, discuss the ideas of the group and decide which characteristics fall into the categories on the charts.

Ideas about girls	Only girls	Some boys	Everyone

Ideas about boys	Only boys	Some girls	Everyone

Copyright © Kate Ripley 2014

7. Not all boys or girls like to do the same things.

Do you know any girls who like to do the same things as boys, or behave like a boy (e.g. watch football on TV)? What do they like to do? How do they behave? For your mission, underline those things that you like to do too.

Do you know any boys who like to do the same things as girls, or behave like a girl (e.g. wear smart clothes)? What do they like to do? How do they behave? For your mission, underline those things that you like to do too.

Theme 9
We Are All Different

1. Feedback from Theme 8 Mission

Share the things you underlined *on your chart* with the group.

2. Look at the things that you do that people may think are boy or girl-type behaviour.

My list	Mostly boys	Mostly girls	Both

We all like different things.

What we like to do does not change whether we are a boy or a girl.

Copyright © Kate Ripley 2014

3. Read about Jane and John.*

Jane is going to secondary school this year. She is in the school football team and likes to watch sport on TV. A lot of her friends are boys and she likes to work with them in class. She thinks the girls who chat about clothes and make-up are pathetic.
- What difficulties might Jane face in Year 7?
- What do you think about Jane? Would you like to be her friend? Would you like to work with her in class?

John is going to secondary school this year. His main interest is cooking and he often prepares meals for the family at home. He is not really interested in sport and spends breaks with a few friends who like to play board games and computer games.
- What difficulties might John face in Year 7?
- What do you think about John? Would you like to be his friend? Would you like to work with him in class?

4. Theme 9 Mission

For the next session bring photographs of yourself:
- aged 0–5
- aged 5–10
- when you first came to _____ school.

Theme 10
We All Grow Up and Change

1. Share your photograph of yourself aged 0–5.

- What could you do when you were _____ years old (e.g. walk, but not climb)?
- What were your interests then?

2. Share your photograph of yourself aged 5–10.
   - Share your next picture with the group.
   - What could you do then that you could not before?
   - What were your interests then?

3. Share your photograph of when you first came to _____ school.
   - What can you do now that you could not do then?
   - What were your interests then?
   - How have you changed since you came to _____ school?

Discuss your ideas with the group.

Record your ideas on the flip chart.

4. Theme 10 Mission

Think about the future. Do you have any ideas about what you will be able to do when you are in Year 11 (aged 15–16)? Fill in the chart about 'When I leave school'.

What will you want to do when you leave school?

When I leave school

I will look like…

I will enjoy…

I will do…

Theme 11
Look into the Future

1. Feedback from Theme 10 Mission
Share ideas about the future using the flip chart.

2. Whatever happened to…?*

Discuss case studies of students who have left _____ school.

Look at pictures of them and discuss what they were doing in Year 10/11 aged 15 or 16 and what they are doing now they have left school.

3. When I am 20 I would like to:

Live: Where? Who with?
Do: Job? College?
In my leisure time I will:
Other new things about me might be:

4. Look again at your pictures.

How has your body changed over time?

Discuss changes with the group and record ideas on the flip chart.

How might your bodies change in the future?

5. Theme 11 Mission

Draw a picture of your ideal self when you leave school.

What will you look like?

What will you like to do?

How will you be different?

When I leave school

I will look like…

I will like…

I will be different because…

PART 2
Puberty and Preparation for Adult Relationships

Theme 12
Understanding our Bodies

> **1. Feedback from Theme 11 Mission**
> Share your pictures and ideas about how you will be when you leave school with the group.

2. Remind students about the Questions Box.

Encourage students to keep using the Questions Box.

3. Explore their understanding of formal and informal names for body parts and processes using the school's sex education materials. Use anatomical dolls or pictures to help the discussions.

Formal names	Informal names (words we use when chatting to friends)
Penis	
Testicles	
Vagina	
Breasts	
Sperm	
Menstruation	
Penetration	
Sex	
Ejaculation	
Masturbation	

What other things have they heard that they are not sure about?

4. How do our bodies change when we go through puberty?

What is puberty?

How do boys change?

How do girls change?

5. Private parts

There are parts of your body that it is usually OK to show to other people. These are areas like your hands, your arms and your eyes.

But there are other parts of your body that it is not OK to show to other people. These are called your 'private parts' or 'sexual parts'. For a man this is his penis and his 'balls' and for a woman this is her vagina and her breasts. For men and women, their bottom or 'bum' is also private.

You should only show your 'private' parts to someone you trust like your doctor or a nurse, your boyfriend or girlfriend.

6. Theme 12 Mission

Think about how your body is changing. If you have any questions, put them in the Questions Box and one of the staff will help you.

Theme 13
Personal Hygiene

1. Feedback from Theme 12 Mission

Is there anything in the Questions Box from the last session that everyone was concerned about that can be discussed as a group?

2. Hygiene

When we grow up we need to be more careful about washing as we tend to sweat more and give off more body odour.

Read about Martin and Natalie.

Martin dislikes a bath or shower and his mother has given up the battle with him so he may not bathe, wash his hair or clean his teeth for more than a week. He often comes to school wearing two pairs of trousers; he sleeps in one and puts on his uniform trousers as well.

- What advice would you give to Martin?
- Plan a hygiene routine to help Martin.

Natalie drives her mother to washing overload. She changes all her clothes and her pyjamas every day. She may change clothing several times during the day as well if there is a mark.

- What advice would you give to Natalie?
- Plan a hygiene routine to help Natalie.

3. Our hygiene routines

Plan a routine with the group using the flip chart.

Morning routine:

Evening routine:

4. My hygiene routine*

Write down what you do each morning and evening. Some things you may need to be reminded about such as brushing your teeth.

Use the highlighter pen to show things that you may forget unless reminded.

Are there some things such as hair washing that you need help with? Write them on your chart too.

- I do…
- I get reminded to do…

Morning:

Evening:

5. What will I need for my daily hygiene routine (e.g. deodorant)?

6. Theme 13 Mission

Complete your 'My daily hygiene routine' chart.

My daily hygiene routine

What I do	Independently	Need help

What will I need (e.g. toothpaste)?

Theme 14
Things People Worry About Around Puberty

1. Feedback from Theme 13 Mission
Share your hygiene routine chart with the group.

2. Masturbation

Can you remember what this word means?

Possible scripts to discuss:

Boys
Rubbing your private parts to make your body feel good. Your penis will go stiff. This is called an erection.

When you reach a climax semen will come out of your penis. This is called ejaculation or 'coming'.

It looks like a milky liquid.

Girls
Rubbing your private parts to make your body feel good. Girls may use their fingers to rub gently around the clitoris area (between your legs at the front). The sensation will build until you reach a climax or orgasm.

Masturbation does not always lead to an orgasm.

This is OK.

Masturbation is a normal healthy activity.

It is OK.

Sometimes people say silly things like it will make you go blind.

This is not true.

Points to remember:

- Masturbation is a private activity. Go to a private place such as your bedroom or the bathroom. People may be upset if you masturbate in public places such as the classroom or sitting room.
- Sometimes you may get excited and want to masturbate when you look at pictures or things on TV. This is normal behaviour for adolescents.
- People do not talk about masturbation except to very close friends.
- If you are worried about masturbation talk to your parents, teacher or doctor.

Remember the Questions Box if you have any questions.

3. 'Wet dreams'

Read Tony's story:

> One morning Tony woke up and found that his bed was wet. He remembered that he used to wet the bed when he was a little boy and how Mum sometimes got cross with him. Tony felt very anxious. He took the sheet off the bed and stuffed it in his wardrobe.
>
> That evening after school, Mum said, 'Tony, where is your sheet? I was going to change the beds today.'

What do you think Tony will say?

Can we help Tony understand what has happened?

Not all boys will have 'wet dreams' but if you do, it is quite normal. Just put your sheet in the washing basket and explain that you needed to change.

4. Skin problems

Some people do get a lot of spots or acne when they are going through puberty. It can make them feel very self-conscious and not want to see or meet people.

- Discuss ideas for self-help (e.g. cleansing routines).
- Consider the pros and cons of getting medication from the GP.

5. Menstruation

When girls become women they start to menstruate.

Can you remember what the word menstruation means?

Possible script to discuss:

> Every month a woman releases an egg from her ovary. Her womb (uterus) prepares its lining to receive a fertilised egg. If she has not had sex so that a man's sperm fertilised the egg, the womb sheds its special lining. This shedding of the lining causes bleeding which lasts four to five days.

Menstruation is often called having your period, your monthlies or 'coming on'.

- Most girls start their periods between 11 and 14 years.
- Before you 'start' you will notice the changes in your body that we talked about in Theme 12.
- Periods are usually irregular for a while until they settle to a regular cycle of 21–32 days.
- Some girls experience 'period pains' or stomach cramps before the bleeding starts and for some hours after.
- Some girls feel low or irritable for a few days before they start a period.
- Girls may choose to use a sanitary pad or a tampon to absorb the blood. (*Making Sense of Sex* by Sarah Attwood, pp.76–85, will give more practical advice about sanitary protection.)
- Periods will stop if a girl is pregnant or if she loses weight to much below 7 stone/95 lbs.

For a girl/mixed group, some discussion about managing 'periods' would be appropriate.

6. Share any other aspects of puberty that the students are worried about or that from experience you know have been concerns in the past.

7. Theme 14 Mission

Remind the students to use the Questions Box; also, to talk to parents about any of the things they are concerned about.

The Mass Debate Quiz

Please answer the following questions, circling the correct answer(s).

1. An erection is:
   (a) a tall building
   (b) when your penis is hard
   (c) when people vote for a new prime minister

2. Masturbation is:
   (a) a private activity
   (b) a public activity

3. Where would you go to masturbate?
   (a) living room
   (b) bathroom
   (c) public toilet
   (d) bedroom

4. I can talk about masturbation to:
   (a) my friends
   (b) teachers
   (c) my doctor
   (d) the class
   (e) my sister
   (f) my brother

5. Ejaculation is:
   (a) when the fire bell sounds and you need to leave the building
   (b) when semen comes out of your penis

6. Semen is:
   (a) a person who goes to sea to catch fish
   (b) the name of a technology company
   (c) milky liquid that comes out of your penis

Thanks to the staff at Robert May's Resource Provision for the quiz.

Copyright © Kate Ripley 2014

Theme 15
Expectations About How We Behave

1. Feedback from Theme 14 Mission
Share any concerns from the Questions Box.

2. Discuss these six situations
As people grow up their behaviour changes. What other people expect of us changes too.

(a) It is Jodie's birthday. She comes downstairs and sees some presents on the table. Jodie jumps up and down, runs to her mum and loudly demands, 'Presents now!' She runs back to the table and starts to rip the paper off the biggest present.

Is the behaviour OK at:	5 years?	10 years?	15 years?

If you were Jodie, what would you do?

What would a friend who was watching think?

(b) John is playing with his cars. His mum calls him to put on his coat to go to the shops. John ignores her. When Mum comes to fetch him he gets very angry and shouts at his mum that he is not going with her.

Is the behaviour OK at:	5 years?	10 years?	15 years?

What would a friend who was watching think?

Does it make a difference if John is making a model that is tricky to do or is in the middle of a computer game?

If you were John, what would you do?

Copyright © Kate Ripley 2014

(c) Beth and her family are going Christmas shopping. The shop is very crowded, so Beth holds her mother's hand.			
Is this behaviour OK at:	5 years?	10 years?	15 years?
If you were Beth, what would you do?			
Beth gets separated from her parents and can't see them in the crush of people. She panics and runs round screaming for her mother, bumping into other shoppers so that she knocks over a little girl. The girl starts crying loudly.			
Is this behaviour OK at:	5 years?	10 years?	15 years?
What would the other shoppers think?			
Would this reaction depend on Beth's age?			
If you were Beth, what would you do?			

(d) Liam is in the front garden clearing up some leaves for his dad. He is fed up with raking leaves. Two boys that he knows walk by and stop to say 'Hello'. One of them says that they are going into town and asks if he would like to come with them. Liam throws down the rake and goes off with the boys.			
Is this behaviour OK at:	5 years?	10 years?	15 years?
Does the age of the boys matter?			
Does how well he knows them matter?			
If you were Liam, what would you do?			

(e) Mike really likes Lisa. She is kind to him and always smiles at him when she sees him. One day he goes up to Lisa and puts his arms round her to give her a hug.			
Is this behaviour OK at:	5 years?	10 years?	15 years?
Does it matter who Lisa is and how he has met her?			

Copyright © Kate Ripley 2014

If you were Mike, what would you do?

(f) Neal has promised that he will go round to Zack's house to play on the computer on Saturday afternoon. Zack is Neal's friend and does not have many friends. On Saturday morning Neal's uncle comes round and asks him if he would like to go to the Motor Show that afternoon. Neal's passion is cars. He goes off with his uncle to the show and forgets about his promise.				
Is this behaviour OK at:		5 years?	10 years?	15 years?
What will Zack think about what has happened?					
If you were Neal, what would you do?					

3. Theme 15 Mission

We all sometimes behave well and at other times blow it.

Next week, keep a log of all the times that you think you behaved in a grown up way when you could have got angry, upset someone or behaved like a younger person.

Date	What I did	What I might have done
	e.g. Kept quiet when the teacher said I was talking.	e.g. Answered back because John had asked me a question.

Theme 16
Behaviour in Public Space and Private Space

1. Feedback from Theme 15 Mission
I behaved in an adult way when…

2. Expectations
- What is public space?
- What is private space?
- Is it always easy to tell?

Sort the Public Space or Private Space Cards into:

| Public Space | Private Space | Not Sure Space |

You may find the idea of Family Space a useful one too.

3. What people do in public and private spaces
What do you think about these pictures?

Copyright © Kate Ripley 2014

4. Situation Cards activity

Sort the Situation Cards into: | Public Space | Private Space | Not Sure Space |

- Are there any times when expectations might be different?
- Can we break the rules?

5. What people wear in public space and private spaces

Sort the Clothing Cards into: | Public Space | Private Space | Family Space |

---

6. Theme 16 Mission

Think of two things that you do now in public space that you will try not to do again from now on (only in private).

1.

2.

Theme 17
Expectations Change

> **1. Feedback from Theme 16 Mission**
> Share 'only in private from now on' ideas with the group.

2. Expectations about hand holding and touching can change.

Expectations at different ages change. Remember Theme 15.

(a) It is common to see parents holding their young children by the hand.

(b) What would you think if you saw a parent holding a teenager by their hand?

(c) Mrs Jones is getting quite unsteady on her feet and uses a stick when she is out walking. She has been to town on the bus. Joe does not know Mrs Jones, but he sees her getting off the bus and holds her hand…

How will Mrs Jones react?

Are there other times when it is OK to touch someone like Joe did?

> Can you think of some times when we might touch someone who we do not really know? Share ideas with the group using the flip chart.

3. Now read John's and Lewis's stories, which concern expectations about nudity.

> John finds some clothes uncomfortable to wear. When he was younger he used to take off all his clothes when he got home from school.
>
> John is now 16. He still likes to take off his clothes but knows not to do this downstairs or outside in the garden. He will go from his room to the bathroom and to the study with no clothes on. His parents have said this is OK. John's sister is coming back from university at the weekend.
> - Does John need to change his habits?
> - His sister's friend is coming too. Does John need to change his habits?
> - What can he do differently?

People behave differently on some occasions. It is Joan's birthday. Lewis does not know her well, but he has been asked to her party. When he arrives, he gives her a hug and says, 'Happy birthday, Joan.'

- How might Joan react?
- Would it be OK for Lewis to hug her when he sees her next day at work?

4. Look at these pictures.

What is happening here?

What about this picture…? What is she doing?

Would this be OK here?

Look at these clothes…

Would it be OK to wear these here?

5. Our relationship to the other person can change expectations.
    (a)   Boyfriends/girlfriends often hold hands. They may hug each other.

(b) James is 15. Miss Lee has been kind to James and helped him with his work. When she comes into the classroom James tries to give her a hug. How will Miss Lee react? What does James need to learn?

(c) People in my life:

I could hold their hand	I should not hold their hand
I could give them a hug	**I should not give them a hug**
Discuss possible exceptions	**Discuss possible exceptions**

5. Theme 17 Mission

Talk to your family.

Are there situations when it is OK to do things that you would not normally do?

Bring two ideas to share at the next session (e.g. Dad crying when the dog died).

Theme 18
What the Law Says

1. Feedback from Theme 17 Mission

Are there situations when it is OK to do things that you would not normally do?

2. Have a guess at what age you can legally do the following:

Activity	Age
Drive a car? Get a provisional licence	
Drive a motor cycle?	
Get a part-time job?	
Be left at home on your own?	
Get married?	
Vote in an election?	
Buy cigarettes in a shop?	
Have sex?	
Order alcohol in a pub?	
Be tried for a crime in court?	

Discussion

- Do you think these ages are the same in other countries?
- Look at the list again. Are there any things on the list that you would not want to do?
- At what age would you want to think of doing some of those things?

3. Draw your own timeline and put on it the things that you want to do and when you think you will feel ready to do them.

```
10 years          20 years          30 years
|        15       |        25       |
```

4. Girlfriends and boyfriends

(a) Some little children talk about having a girlfriend/boyfriend. They may sit together, or even hold hands. Some children are teased about their girlfriend/boyfriend.

> Richard likes to sit next to Lisa in maths. She is good at it and helps him. They sometimes play tag on the playground with some other children or eat their lunch together. Mary teases Lisa about her 'boyfriend'.

(b) Some people start 'going out' with a boy or girl in Year 7 (aged 11 or 12).
- What does 'going out' with someone mean?
- What sort of things might they do?

Share ideas with the group using the flip chart.
- How is it different from the story about Lisa and Richard?

Share ideas with the group using the flip chart.

(c) Some people do not have a boyfriend/girlfriend at school but find someone they like at college or at work. This is OK. We are all different.

5. Some things that people you know do may not be legal.
- Posing for pictures without your clothes on and uploading them to Facebook if you are under 16 years old.
- Getting together to watch a pornographic film.

If you were asked by friends to do these things, what would you say/do?

6. If you could do any activities you wanted to, that are not on the previous list, at what age would you like to try them (e.g. fly an aeroplane, go on holiday without your family).

To do list	Age

7. Theme 18 Mission
Add to your list of things that you would like to do. Can you find out more about the law in other countries (e.g. the age for buying alcohol in the USA)?

Theme 19
Making Friends

1. Feedback from Theme 18 Mission

What things would you like to do when you are older?

What did you find out about the law in other countries?

2. Making friends

Do you remember some of your ideas from Theme 6?

3. Top tips for making friends:
- Get them talking.
- Listen to what they say.
- Make them feel important, liked.
- Find things you have in common.

4. Get them talking

Opening gambits: What could you say?

(Remember to smile and look at the other person before speaking.)

- *Scenario:* It is Monday morning and you meet Wendy as you get off the bus…

Share ideas with the group using the flip chart.

- *Scenario:* It is after break and John sits in the seat next to you, hot and red in the face, still clutching his tennis racquet…

Share ideas with the group using the flip chart.

- *Scenario:* You are on your way out and you see Wendy looking under the tables with an anxious expression on her face…

Share ideas with the group using the flip chart.

- *Scenario:* You are waiting for your bus, which is late, and so is John who is standing next to you…

Share ideas with the group using the flip chart.

Practise some of these opening gambits in the group.

What other things can you say to open a conversation…

- when you come into your tutor group?
- when you join your class group?
- at lunch time?

5. Talking and listening

Play the reporter game in the group.

In pairs, students take turns to ask each other about what they like or do. Topics might include: their family, hobbies, favourite TV programmes, best holiday, etc.

The students report back to the group about what the other person said.

6. Theme 19 Mission

Start a conversation with someone you do not know well.

Name the person.

When will you try to start the conversation?

What will you say? Practise with the group.

Next time: report back. How did it go?

Making Friends

Do you remember some of the things that help us to make friends?
- Look at them and smile.
- Ask them about themselves.
- Listen to what they say and respond to that (maintain the topic).
- Take equal turns in the conversation.
- Explore things you both like/are interested in.
- When it feels safe to do so, share some personal thoughts and feelings.

Theme 20
Being a Friend

1. Feedback from Theme 19 Mission
Who did you start a conversation with?

What result did you get?

2. About Me

Use the About Me Cards to do a card sorting activity. Sort the cards into three piles:

| Like me | Sometimes like me | Not me |

3. What would a friend do?

Students take turns to pick up a Response Card and decide with the help of the group what the friendly response to each situation would be.

4. We often show friendship by what we do as well as what we say.

What can we do to be kind and helpful to other people (e.g. give a compliment)?

Discuss what they have done/might do and record the ideas on a flip chart.

5. Theme 20 Mission

Keep an Acts of Friendship Log for the week.

What did you do to be a friend each day (e.g. helped Jane to find her trainers, let Bob share my book)?

Acts of Friendship Log

Week beginning:	Monday
	Who?
	Where?
	What I did

Tuesday	Wednesday
Who?	Who?
Where?	Where?
What I did	What I did

Thursday	Friday
Who?	Who?
Where?	Where?
What I did	What I did

Saturday	Sunday
Who?	Who?
Where?	Where?
What I did	What I did

Copyright © Kate Ripley 2014

Theme 21
From Friendships to Relationships*

---

1. Feedback from Theme 20 Mission

Discuss the acts of friendship from the students' friendship logs.

---

2. Teenagers often talk about girlfriends/boyfriends, but people start 'dating', or having a girlfriend/boyfriend, at different ages – when they feel ready and are attracted to someone.

Do you feel that you 'should' have a girlfriend/boyfriend?

Discuss why the students feel that way. Record responses on a flip chart.

3. Attraction
- How do you know?
- How do you feel?

Discuss what we have learned from books, films and our own experiences.

We will use the symbol ♥ for the person we are attracted to.

Share ideas with the group using the flip chart.

Attracted to ♥

How you might feel:

What you might do:

---

4. Theme 21 Mission

John 'fancies' Jane.

There will be someone in your class who 'fancies' a girl or boy.

What do they do to try to get noticed by their ♥?

Watch them, listen to what they say.

What can you learn from other people?

Theme 22

Things Are Not Always What They Seem

1. Feedback from Theme 21 Mission

What do people do and say when they 'fancy' someone? What did you learn from your observations?

2. Things are not always what they seem

Before and after airbrushing/digital enhancement:

3. Spot the difference*

Look at pictures of ordinary people and people in the media. See if you can spot the difference.

4. Attraction or hero worship?

Wanting to be like someone – hero worship – is something most boys and girls experience. It may be someone we know or someone on TV.

Copyright © Kate Ripley 2014

We might try to behave like them, go to places they go, try to make friends.

Some young people may confuse hero worship with physical/sexual attraction.

---

5. Theme 22 Mission
Complete the chart below.

My ideal girlfriend/boyfriend would:

Like to: (think of things you like to do)

Be: (what qualities would you hope for, e.g. kind/clever)

Look like:

Theme 23
Thinking About a Relationship

1. Feedback from Theme 22 Mission
Discuss ideal boyfriend/girlfriend ideas from last week.

Collate the ideas on the flip chart.

They would like to…
(interests and hobbies)

They would be…
(qualities, e.g. kind)

They would look like…

2. Making ourselves attractive to ♥

What can we do?

Appearance:

Personal hygiene:

Behaviour:

Discuss ideas with the group.

3. How do we learn what to do?

You have all been involved with the sex education programme at your school which teaches students some of the basic facts about relationships and sex. We all pick up other information from other sources. Some of these are on the list.

- Put a tick by the sources that you have found helpful.
- Now rank them. Number 1 is the source that you have found the most helpful.

Source of information	Helpful information	Rank
Mum		
Dad		
A friend		
A brother or sister		
Teacher/lesson		
Watching films		
Reading book		
Magazines		
TV		
Internet		

4. Not all of the information is true.

Are these statements True or False?

Statement	True	False
1. You can get pregnant by kissing.		
2. Masturbation can make you go blind.		
3. A condom will protect you from sexually transmitted diseases.		
4. You can't get pregnant the first time you have sex.		
5. You need to be married to have a baby.		
6. You have to have sex if you have a girl/boyfriend.		
7. Using cling-film is as good as a condom.		
8. You can't marry your aunt.		
9. If you masturbate you are gay.		
10. Some people are not very interested in sex.		

5. Theme 23 Mission

Write down any other things that you wonder if they are true or not, and bring them to our next session, or put them in the Questions Box.

Theme 24
Eat Well and Be Healthy

---

1. Feedback from Theme 23 Mission
What 'facts' did you wonder about? Discuss your True or False answers with the group using the flip chart.

---

2. Food in → energy out

$F > E =$ ☹

Eat more food than you need = get fat

$F < E =$ ☹

Eat less food than you need = get thin

$F = E =$ ☺

The Goldilocks balance = just right

Discuss the implications for health and fitness

3. Read about Sam.

Sam lives on his own in a flat and walks to work. One day when he visited his mum he said he needed to buy new work trousers. 'But you bought some a few months ago,' said his mum. 'They are too tight now,' replied Sam. Sam was putting on weight although he said he only ate one meal a day. Sam and his mum found out:

- Sam was eating lots of snacks: chocolate bars and crisps, but not 'counting' them as 'food in'.
- Sam was not eating balanced meals.
- Sam was mostly sitting at his computer when he was not at work.

What advice can we offer Sam and his mum?

Sam does not like sport or taking much exercise, but he likes facts and figures.

4. Being overweight can affect your health but so can being too thin. Read about Gary.

> Gary had never liked trying new foods. When he was a little boy he only ate toast and marmite and crisps. As he got older he tried a few more foods but had the same things most days. His mum was worried because he would not eat any vegetables or fruit except for apples. Gary was always saying that he was tired. He found it hard to get up in the mornings and his school grades were getting worse. He used to like going for bike rides with his brother but he now said this was 'boring'. His mum took him to the doctor who said Gary was too thin.

What advice can we offer Gary and his mum?

5. Read about Jancis.

> Jancis was worried about going to school because she thought people were saying unkind things behind her back and she was finding the work hard. Her sister who had always stuck up for her had left school to go to college so Jancis felt that she had no-one to confide in. Jancis started to throw her packed lunch away because she did not feel like eating. In the evening, she found ways of hiding how little she ate at home. Jancis noticed that her 'periods' were no longer regular and eventually they stopped altogether. She knew she could not be pregnant…

What has happened to Jancis?

What advice would we give to Jancis and her mum?

6. Theme 24 Mission

Find out your height and weight. How many calories a day do you need? Give the group a chart to work this out. Stress that the figures are only a guide. Is your balance about right?

Keep a food log of all you eat and drink each day for a week. Remember, sweets and snacks count!

Can you find the Goldilocks balance for you?

What might you do to get your Goldilocks balance?

Theme 25
A Balanced Diet

1. Feedback from Theme 24 Mission
You measured your height and weight. Do you think you have the Goldilocks balance for you? Remember the charts are only guidelines – we can be safely about 10lbs more or less than the average. Do you need to change what you eat or what you do?

2. A balanced diet?

- We need to eat some of each food group to be healthy: fats, carbohydrates, proteins.
- We also need vitamins and minerals. A balanced diet gives most people all they need.
- Health advisors also say we should eat five portions of fruit and vegetables each day.
- Which foods do you know that have fats, carbohydrates and proteins? List them on the flip chart.
- Look at your food log.

3. As a group, write on the flip chart all the foods that are in the food logs.

Put the foods onto cards, for example: | biscuits |

Now sort the cards into the food groups where they belong:

Carbohydrates	Fats	Protein
	biscuits	

Look on food packet labels to help you decide where they go if you are not sure.

4. Five a day?

- Look at your food log.
- How many portions of fruit and vegetables did you eat each day of the week?
- Draw a graph for the group to see on average how many portions a day everyone had.
- What fruit/vegetables are most popular in the group?

5. Theme 25 Mission

Look at what fruit and vegetables other people in the group like. Name one new fruit or vegetable that you will try before the next session.

Theme 26
Getting to Know You

1. Feedback from Theme 25 Mission

Which new fruit or vegetable did you try?

Will you eat it regularly in the future?

If you did not like that one, which one will you try next?

2. So if you 'fancy' someone, what can you do?

- Share the same space.

If ♥ always gets to the tutor room early, you could do the same.

If ♥ always eats in the _____, you could do the same.

What else might you do?

Share ideas with the group, for example join the same club.

- Find out what they like and like to do.

How might you do this?

- Share ideas with the group, for example watch/listen to…

3. Health warning: do they really like the same things as you?

> Kate really liked Chris, who was mad about cricket. They worked together in science class and had fun. Every Saturday and two nights a week in the summer, Chris played cricket. Kate hated cricket and got bored watching Chris play…
> - Is this relationship likely to last?

Be realistic – do you want to talk about X-Factor all the time, or go to concerts by ♥'s favourite band if you can't stand them?

Do you have mutual friends, friends in common?

They might:
- introduce you
- help you share the same space
- put in a good word for you.

Boy or girl friends that you have can be useful to help you get to know ♥.

4. A true friend?

> Sally tells Lizzie that she really likes Paul. She asks her to keep it a secret. Lizzie says that Paul is a friend of her brother's and often comes round to her house after school. Lizzie invites Sally to come home with her the next day, so that they can do homework together.

- Is Lizzie being a good friend?
- Has Lizzie really invited Sally to her house to do homework?
- What might happen next?

5. Can you trust everyone?

Sally tells Jenny that she really likes Paul and asks her not to tell anyone else. The next morning at school, Mary says in a loud voice, 'Look, your boyfriend has just come in.'

- How does Mary know?
- Was Jenny a good friend?
- How do you think Paul and Sally feel?

6. Acts of friendship

Look again at your Acts of Friendship Log from Theme 20.

What things might you do to help you get to know someone better?

Discuss ideas with the group, for example help with homework, setting up a website.

Acts of friendship that help to build a relationship:

7. Theme 26 Mission

Practise two of the acts of friendship you have identified.

How did the other person respond?

Brush Up on Your Conversational Skills

Starting a conversation.

Opening gambit.

Non-verbal behaviour.

Choosing a subject to talk about.

What they like, ask them about it.

↓

Monitor their response – are they interested or should you change the subject?

↓

Listen to them, make them feel important.

End the conversation politely.

In groups of three, practise a conversation.
- Person 1 opens the conversation.
- Person 2 responds.
- Person 3 checks what you do.

Swap roles.

Copyright © Kate Ripley 2014

Check Sheet

Did I...?

	✓
Smile.	
Look at person 2.	
Choose a good opening gambit.	
Choose a subject that 2 is interested in.	
Listen well.	
Look at 2 and monitor level of interest.	
End the conversation politely.	
Or change to another topic smoothly.	
Say something positive to make 2 feel good.	

Theme 27
Reading the Hidden Messages

1. Feedback from Theme 26 Mission

Discuss the acts of friendship the students tried out and the responses they had.

How did the responses make them feel?

Making relationships and getting close to someone is hard for all young people, and for adults too. Coping when relationships do not work out is upsetting whoever you are.

The message is to take it slowly. Read the messages from ♥.

♥ may be comfortable with occasional help with something practical but not be ready to or want to move on.

2. What is the message?

Hugh and Janet

Hugh has helped Janet with some IT work in the lesson. She has thanked him and seems grateful.

Hugh: 'Would you like to finish it off at lunch time?'

Janet: 'Sorry, I have dance club.'

Hugh: 'What about tomorrow?'

Janet: 'I'm not sure what I am doing tomorrow.'

- What is Janet really saying to Hugh?
- Would it have been different if Janet had said, 'Sorry, I have dance club, what about tomorrow?'
- What might Janet have really been saying to Hugh in that case?

Nick and Sarah

Nick and his friends have been talking about a film that they have seen advertised. Nick says he would really like to see it. Sarah is part of the group. She walks with Nick as they go off to lessons and says, 'I haven't seen the film yet, have you?'

Nick: 'No.'

Sarah: 'Would you like to go on Friday? I think it finishes at the weekend.'

Nick: 'I am going shopping on Friday.'

Sarah: 'What about Saturday then?'

Nick: 'I am baby-sitting Saturday.'

- What message is Nick giving?
- Does he want to see the film?
- What would Nick think if Sarah kept on asking him to go to a film with her?

Some messages are non-verbal

A group of friends go outside to eat lunch.

John sits next to Sally on a wall. He opens a bag of crisps and offers Sally some.

She smiles at him, takes a few and says 'thank you'. John moves closer to Sally so that their shoulders and knees are touching. Sally moves away.

- What is the message Sally is giving?
- Would the message be different if Sally had not moved away?

3. Recognising the 'brush off'

Louise and Ted

Louise came to a club with two girl friends. She met Ted at the club. They danced together and Ted bought Louise a drink. At the end of the evening, Louise joined her girl friends and they started to put on their coats. Ted asked for Louise's email but she said 'Give me yours'. Ted kept checking his computer but there was no email from Louise.

- Why did Louise not give Ted her email?
- Did Louise intend to contact Ted?

Examples of 'brush off' phrases:
- I'm washing my hair that night.
- I have to go out with my mum.
- I've got too much homework.
- My phone was stolen and I lost all my numbers.
- I'm busy that night…ooh, and that night too…
- I did have your number, but the dog must have eaten it!

4. Theme 27 Mission

Can you think of any other 'brush off' phrases that you have heard? Ask your family and friends what 'brush offs' they would use.

If the real message is 'I am not interested in getting to know you better', move on. Forget it. We all have lots of false starts before we get it right.

Theme 28
It Takes Two: Dealing with Setbacks

> **1. Feedback from Theme 27 Mission**
> Discuss any 'brush off' phrases they have heard.

2. You may like someone a lot and want to be with them. If they do not feel the same way the friendship/relationship will not work.

- How will I feel if they do not feel the same?
- What will I do if they do not feel the same?
- Collate ideas on the flip chart.

3. Read the following stories.

> **Paul**
>
> Paul really liked Leanne. One evening he walked home with her after college and thought she might like him. Paul waited for Leanne after college the next day. She was with a group of friends. Paul followed the group to Leanne's house. The same thing happened the next day. On the fourth day, one of Leanne's friends said, 'Push off, creep!' Paul started to follow Leanne around at college and to wait outside her home at weekends. Leanne's dad came out and said he would call the police if Paul did not leave his daughter alone.

- Where did Paul go wrong? What messages did he not read?
- What would you do if you were Paul?

Harry

Harry liked Claire who was in his tutor group. He tried to sit by her in the mornings and she always said 'Hello' and smiled at him. One day he found out that she liked JLS and brought her his CDs to borrow. Claire said thank you, but she had most of them already. She avoided him when he tried to sit by her the next day. Harry felt very angry. He wrote a note about how he wanted to kill Claire. His teacher found the note.

- Where did Harry go wrong?
- Did Harry really want to kill Claire?
- What might people think about Harry?
- What would you do if you were Harry?

4. Think of a time when you have been disappointed or 'let down' such as when you were unable to go on a trip you were looking forward to, or when a friend said they would call you, and they didn't.

What did you do to make yourself feel better?

Share ideas on the flip chart.

5. Theme 28 Mission

Think of some more things that you do to feel better when you are sad or angry. What works for you? Bring one idea to the next session.

Theme 29
Building a Relationship

> ### 1. Feedback from Theme 28 Mission
> Collate ideas for things that make members of the group feel better on the flip chart.
>
> Key questions to ask:
> 1. What is my relationship with this person?
> 2. Do they have the same feelings?
>
> We have to keep in step, like in a dance.

2. Mirror work

Students work in pairs. One is the leader and the other is the reflection. The leader moves and the reflection follows the movements, without touching the other.

Swap roles.

The aim is to keep in step. The game illustrates how the leader has to wait for the partner to respond before moving on to make the next move.

3. Distance and relationships

Find some pictures of people who you meet at school and in the community, for example a doctor, a policeman, a postman, a teacher, a shop assistant, and find some more pictures of your friends and family. You might want to make masks or dress up as the characters. Use the pictures or role play to decide how close you might stand when talking to these people. Discuss ideas about personal space and what feels comfortable to you and to them.

4. Card sorting activity

Sort the Personal Space cards into the three categories below.

What rules apply?

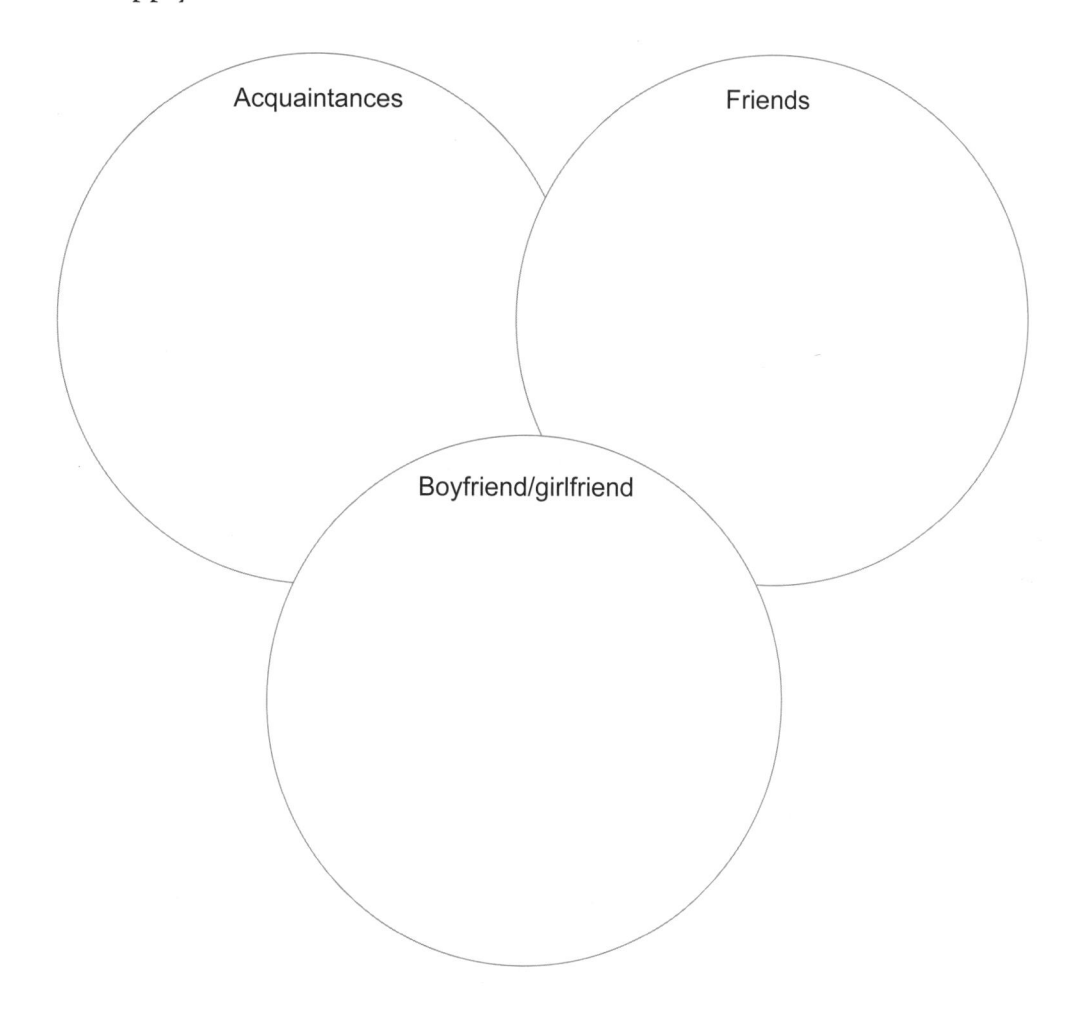

- Acquaintances
- Friends
- Boyfriend/girlfriend

In what situations might the rules change (e.g. in a dance class you might hold hands with an acquaintance)?

5. Card sorting activity

Sort the Actions Cards into actions for Private Space only, Public or Private Space.

In what situations might the rules change?

6. Theme 29 Mission

Points to ponder about relationships:

- Not everyone wants to be in a close relationship. That is OK.
- A relationship may lead to a physical/sexual relationship, or it may not. That is OK.
- Most boys want a relationship with a girl. Most girls want a relationship with a boy. They are called heterosexual. That is OK.
- Some boys or girls want a relationship with a person of the same sex. They are called homosexual. That is OK.
- Some men and women may choose to get married. Some same sex partners may choose a civil partnership. Both are equal under the law.

Theme 30
Safe Sex

> **1. Feedback from Theme 29 Mission**
> Discuss the 'points to ponder' about relationships.

You have found someone who is attractive to you and ♥ feels the same way about you. You would like to start a physical relationship with ♥.

2. Safety first: emotional safety

Trying something new is scary. Most people are anxious before their first sexual experience. We worry about all sorts of things.

- Will ♥ be put off by my body because I do not look like people in the media and films?
- Will it hurt?
- Will ♥ gossip about what we have done?
- Will I do it right and satisfy ♥?

Discuss other concerns that the students have.

A key question to ask: Do I trust ♥?

3. Safety first: sensory needs

You may already be aware that you are sensitive to some lighting levels, sounds, smells, or textures that make you feel uncomfortable. For example, some people dislike strong perfumes/aftershave, or prefer a firm touch to gently stroking.

Fill in the sensory chart to help you identify what would make you feel comfortable.

Sensory chart

Sense	Like	Find uncomfortable
Lighting/colours		
Sounds		
Smells		
Touch		
Taste		
Textures		

Discuss the sensory preferences of the group.

Everyone is different and has different needs. One person's mood music may set ♥'s teeth on edge.

You and ♥ will be more relaxed if you talk about what you do or do not like.

4. Your choice

A sexual relationship makes you feel good if you are with someone who you find attractive, trust, find fun to be with – and you feel relaxed in their company.

Sometimes people who do not really value you may put pressure on you to have sex with them.

They might say things like:
- Everyone does it.
- You would do it if you really loved me.
- I will dump you if you won't.
- You are just scared.

What other things might people say to try to persuade you to have sex?

Would you trust people who say these things?

It is your choice to say NO.

5. How often?

If you are in a relationship you may worry about how often you should have sex. There is no rule about how often people in a relationship should have sex. Some people have sex often, once a day or more, particularly at the start of a relationship. Other people are not very interested in having sex. We are all different. However, a relationship is often stronger if you and your partner feel the same about how often to have sex.

6. Physical safety: sexually transmitted diseases (STDs)

Have you heard of STDs?

Which ones have you heard of?

Possible script to discuss:

> Some STDs can be potentially life-threatening, like HIV which can lead to AIDS. The person carrying the infection may not know because there are no obvious physical symptoms. Chlamydia is another infection that has no physical symptoms in men but may cause infertility in women. Your partner may not be aware that they carry an infection.
>
> Other infections may have physical symptoms like genital warts or cause a discharge. Most people consult their GP if they experience any of these symptoms but they could still infect a partner until the infection is cleared up.
>
> The only safe way to avoid STDs is to use a condom.

Discuss:

- Where can condoms be purchased?
- Can condoms be re-used?
- Can other things be used as condoms?
- Are there any other ways of avoiding infections (some people opt for abstinence)?

7. Physical safety: contraception

Many young people are sexually active before they are in a long term relationship or plan to have a baby. Girls are fertile from when they have their first period and boys when they start to produce sperm. There is a chance of pregnancy when sperm comes near to the vulva even when penetration has not taken place.

There are many forms of contraception available.

Discuss with the students what is available using the flip chart.

Methods of contraception	Men	Women	Effectiveness	High	Medium	Low
Oral contraception (the pill)						
Intrauterine devices (the coil)						
Condoms						
Hormone injections (3 monthly)						
Rhythm method						
Morning After Pill (emergencies only)						

Tell the students the following facts:
- The pill is 98% effective if used correctly.
- Condoms are 85–88% effective if used correctly.

Discuss the advantages and disadvantages of the methods and contraception that are available.

8. Another look into the future

In Theme 11 we shared ideas about what you might be like when you were 20 years old and had left school.

Since then we have talked much more about becoming an adult; the body changes that come with puberty and how to build relationships.

Complete the 'This Is Me at 20' chart.

Compare your responses at the end of the course with the responses you made in Theme 11.

Discuss the changes in your group.

This Is Me at 20

Where will I live?
Who will I live with?

What will I do?
Job? College?

In my leisure time, I will enjoy…

I would like to have:
A car?
A girl/boyfriend?
Pets?
What other things would you like to have?

Appendix 1
Tutor Notes

Theme 1: This Is Me

The photocopiable materials in this session are to be used as the focus for discussions, rather than as worksheets for the students to complete in isolation.

Activity 1: Guess who?

For this activity you will need pictures of famous people from magazines or the internet.

Activity 3: My interests

Collate the ideas from 'What I like to do' and 'What I really do not like' on a flip chart so that the students can see who has similar likes and dislikes to them. Discuss ideas using the flip chart.

Mission

Make part one of the Mission more demanding by:

- increasing the number of people
- increasing the number of interests
- working with different teaching groups.

Theme 2: Me and My World
Mission

Students will need a copy of the family tree they have made to take home for this mission.

Theme 3: Friendships
Activity 3: Card sorting activity

This is done as a whole group to prompt discussion. Add any more ideas that come from the group to your set of cards.

Activity 4: My friend

This is a group discussion activity. Collate ideas from the group on the flip chart.

Theme 5: Who Do I Trust?

Introduction to students:

'In the first four sessions we talked about family and friends. They can help us when we have a problem and teachers may be able to help too.'

Activity 2: Who would I trust?

This activity is more fun for the students if the prompts 1–10 are written on cards and the students discuss their ideas in the group. This activity can be made into a card game. Students turn up one card at a time and say who they would trust. Others in the group are invited to say who they would trust. Alternatively, read out the prompts and the students say who their choice would be.

Theme 6: Making Friends
Activity 2: Circle of friends

The students fill in the chart themselves first. Their ideas are then shared on the flip chart. You may need to explain what they need to do and give examples of who might go in some of the circles.

Theme 9: We Are All Different
Activity 3: Read about Jane and John

Discuss the case studies of Jane and John as a group.
Aim to explore the gender constancy issue, i.e. that Jane is still a girl even though she likes boy-type activities and dresses like a boy.
Aim to explore how not conforming to gender stereotypes does not mean they are 'gay'.
Explore terminology. Remind the students about the Questions Box here.
Some prompt questions:

- Do you know any girls like Jane? Do you know any boys like John?
- Would you choose to be their friend? Explore reasons why.
- What do you think people might say about Jane/John behind their backs?
- What do you think Jane/John might be like as adults?

Theme 11: Look into the Future
Activity 2: Whatever happened to…?

Prepare two short case studies of students with AS who have left school, preferably students that they have known. If possible, you might invite a student who has left to come back to talk to the group.

Theme 13: Personal Hygiene
Activity 4: My hygiene routine

Some students may need additional help with hygiene. A useful resource is the book *Personal Hygiene? What's That Got to Do with Me?* by Pat Crissey (Jessica Kingsley Publishers, 2006).

Theme 21: From Friendships to Relationships

It may be helpful for the students to read and discuss quotes from teenage literature. Alternatively you may prefer to share clips from films or television.

Suggestions for books to read

Gibbons, A. (2001) *Julie and Me…and Michael Owen Makes Three.* London: Orion Books.

Kennedy, L.E. (2007) *My Best Friend's Brother.* London: Piccadilly Press Ltd.

McCombie, K. (2002) *My Funny Valentine.* London: Scholastic Children's Books.

Langham, T. (1998) *A Boy Like That.* London: A and C Black.

Theme 22: Things Are Not Always What They Seem
Activity 3: Spot the difference

You will need to find pictures of celebrities and ordinary people from magazines or the internet for use in this exercise.

Appendix 2
Baseline Assessments

Growing up (boys)

How much do you agree with the following statements?

1 = Not like me   3 = A bit like me   5 = Like me

1. I am looking forward to being an adult.
   1 — 2 — 3 — 4 — 5

2. I understand how my body will change as a grown up.
   1 — 2 — 3 — 4 — 5

3. I feel confident to ask someone when I feel worried about growing up.
   1 — 2 — 3 — 4 — 5

4. I am comfortable speaking about things to do with sex.
   1 — 2 — 3 — 4 — 5

5. I sometimes think I am different from other boys.
   1 — 2 — 3 — 4 — 5

6. I am able to make new friends.
   1 — 2 — 3 — 4 — 5

7. I am comfortable when I am with other boys.
   1 — 2 — 3 — 4 — 5

8. I am comfortable when I am with girls.
   1 — 2 — 3 — 4 — 5

9. Other people think I behave differently from other boys.
   1 — 2 — 3 — 4 — 5

10. I prefer to work and play on my own.
    1 — 2 — 3 — 4 — 5

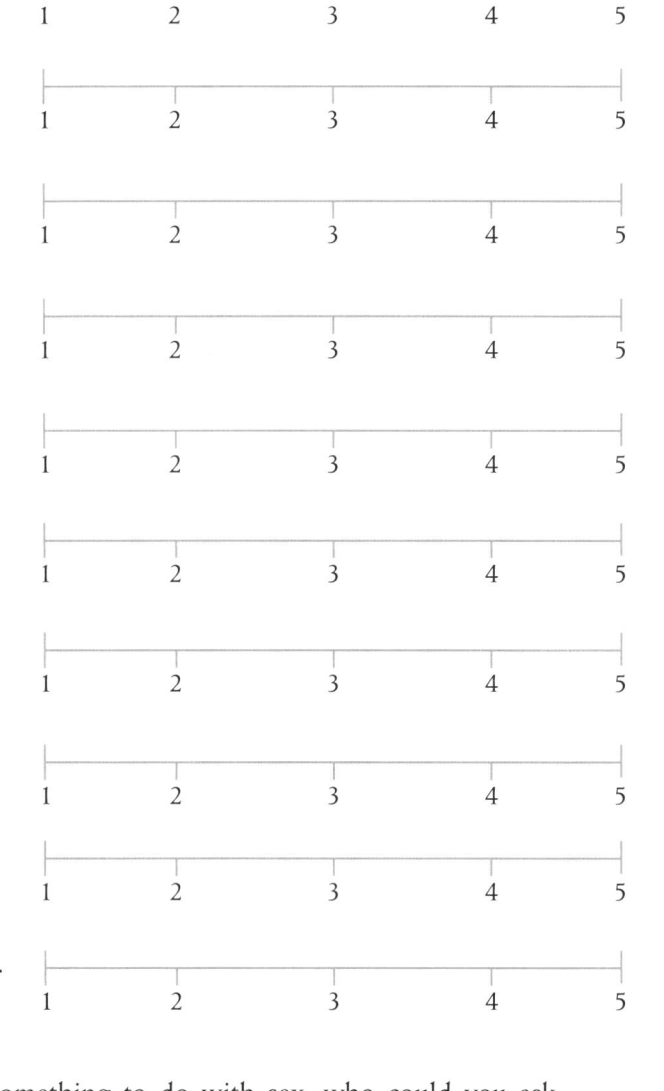

If you were worried about growing up and something to do with sex, who could you ask for help?

Copyright © Kate Ripley 2014

Growing up (girls)

How much do you agree with the following statements?

1 = Not like me   3 = A bit like me   5 = Like me

1. I am looking forward to being an adult.

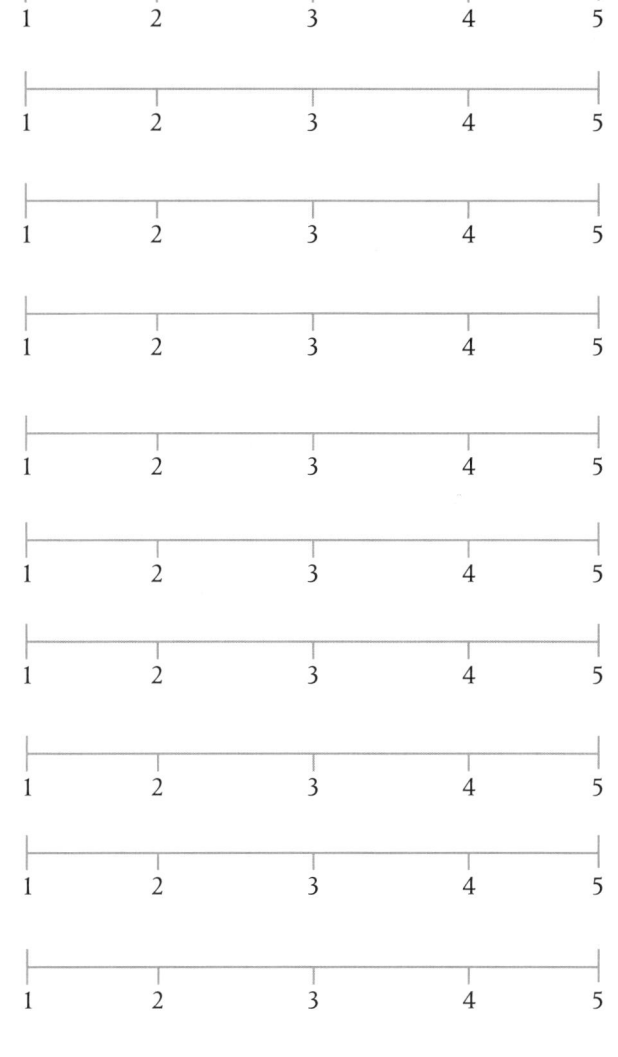

   1   2   3   4   5

2. I understand how my body will change as a grown up.

   1   2   3   4   5

3. I feel confident to ask someone when I feel worried about growing up.

   1   2   3   4   5

4. I am comfortable speaking about things to do with sex.

   1   2   3   4   5

5. I sometimes think I am different from other girls.

   1   2   3   4   5

6. I am able to make new friends.

   1   2   3   4   5

7. I am comfortable when I am with other girls.

   1   2   3   4   5

8. I am comfortable when I am with boys.

   1   2   3   4   5

9. Other people think I behave differently from other girls.

   1   2   3   4   5

10. I prefer to work and play on my own.

    1   2   3   4   5

If you were worried about growing up and something to do with sex, who could you ask for help?

Copyright © Kate Ripley 2014

Definitions and colloquialisms for sexual terms

1. Puberty	
2. Ejaculation	
3. Vagina	
4. Pubic hair	
5. Sperm	
6. Ovulation	

When they are chatting, people do not always call parts of the body or other things to do with sex by their formal names. What other words or phrases might we use for:

7. Penis	
8. Testicles	
9. Breasts	
10. Pregnancy	

Gender stereotypes

Who does what?

Boys/Men?   or   Girls/Women?

1. Who usually watches football on TV? _____
   - (a) Is it wrong for the other gender to watch football?   Y / N
   - (b) Would it be OK for you to watch football?   Y / N
   - (c) Would you like to be friends with a girl who liked football?   Y / N
   - (d) Would you be worried if you liked watching football?   Y / N

2. Who usually does the ironing in the home? _____
   - (a) Is it wrong for the other gender to do the ironing?   Y / N
   - (b) Would it be OK for you to do the ironing?   Y / N
   - (c) Would you like to be friends with a boy who liked doing the ironing?   Y / N
   - (d) Would you be worried if you liked doing the ironing?   Y / N

3. Who usually has long hair? _____
   - (a) Is it wrong for the other gender to have long hair?   Y / N
   - (b) Would it be OK for you to have long hair?   Y / N
   - (c) Would you like to be friends with a boy who had long hair?   Y / N
   - (d) Would you be worried if you wanted long hair?   Y / N

4. Who usually likes to go dancing? _____
   - (a) Is it wrong for the other gender to enjoy dancing?   Y / N
   - (b) Would it be OK for you to go dancing?   Y / N
   - (c) Would you like to be friends with a boy who liked dancing?   Y / N
   - (d) Would you be worried if you enjoyed dancing?   Y / N

5. Who usually wears nail polish? _____
   - (a) Is it wrong for the other gender to wear nail polish?   Y / N
   - (b) Would it be OK for you to wear nail polish?   Y / N
   - (c) Would you like to be friends with a boy who wore nail polish?   Y / N
   - (d) Would you be worried if you liked wearing nail polish?   Y / N

Personal constructs

Personal constructs are elicited from young people to help understand their perspective about themselves and their lives. For the pilot study this part of the baseline assessment was carried out by an educational psychologist in training who had studied the personal construct theory and practice.

If users of the programme wish to use this technique as part of a baseline assessment, it is recommended that they first attend a practitioners' course in eliciting personal constructs.

To find out more about personal constructs:

Ravenette, T. (1999) *Personal Construct Theory in Educational Psychology: A Practitioner View*. Oxford: Wiley-Blackwell.

Butler, R. and Green, D.R. (2007) *The Child Within: Taking the Young Person's Perspective by Applying Personal Construct Psychology*. Oxford: Wiley-Blackwell.

Burnham, S. (2008) *Let's Talk: Using Personal Construct Psychology to Support Children and Young People*. London: Sage.

References

Baron-Cohen, S. (2002) 'The extreme male brain theory of autism.' *Trends in Cognitive Sciences, 6*, 248–254.

Coe, J. (2011) 'Gender identity and sexuality issues in young people with autism spectrum disorder.' Unpublished thesis, University of Southampton.

de Lisi, R. and Johns, M.L. (1984) 'The effects of books and gender constancy development on kindergarten children's sex-role attitudes.' *Journal of Applied Psychology, 5*, 173–184.

de Vries, A.L.C., Noens, I.L.J., Cohen-Kettenis, P.T., Van Berckelaer-Onnes, I.A. and Doreleijers, T.A. (2010) 'Autism spectrum disorders in gender dysphoric children and adolescents.' *Journal of Autism and Development Disorders, 40*, 930–936.

Gomez de la Cuesta, G. and Mason, J. (2010) *Asperger's Syndrome for Dummies.* Chichester: John Wiley and Sons Ltd.

Kohlberg, L. (1966) 'A Cognitive-Developmental Analysis of Children's Sex Role Concepts and Attitudes.' In E.E. Maccoby (ed.) *The Development of Sex Differences.* Stanford, CA: Stanford University Press.

Koller, R. (2000) 'Sexuality and adolescents with autism.' *Sexuality and Disability, 18*, 125–135.

Lawson, W. (2005) *Sex, Sexuality and the Autism Spectrum.* London: Jessica Kingsley Publishers.

Mucaddes, N.M. (2002) 'Gender identity problems in autistic children.' *Child Care Health and Development 28*, 6, 529–532.

National Children's Bureau (2003) *Talk to Your Children About Sex and Relationships: Support for Parents. Forum Fact Sheet 32.* National Children's Bureau Sex Education Forum.

Ravenette, T. (1999) *Personal Construct Theory in Educational Psychology: A Practitioner View.* Weinheim: Wiley.

Ruble, D.N., Taylor, L.J., Cyphers, L., Greulich, F.K., Lurye, L.E. and Shrout, P.E. (2007) 'The role of gender constancy in early gender development.' *Child Development, 78*, 4, 1121–1136.

Ruble, L. and Dalrymple, N. (1993) 'Social/sexual awareness of persons with autism: a parental perspective.' *Archives of Sexual Behaviour, 22*, 229–240.

Sicile-Kira, C. (2006) *Adolescents on the Autism Spectrum.* New York: The Berkley Publishing Group.

Signorella, M.L., Bigler, R.S. and Liben, L.S. (1993) 'Developmental differences in children's gender schemata about others. A meta analytic review.' *Developmental Review, 13*, 147–183.

Slaby, R.E. and Frey, K.S. (1975) 'Development of gender constancy and selective attention to same sex models.' *Child Development, 46*, 849–856.

Stokes, M., Newton, N. and Kaur, A. (2007) 'Stalking, and social and romantic functioning among adolescents and adults with autism spectrum disorder'. *Journal of Autism and Developmental Disorders, 37*, 1969–1986.

Tissot, C. (2009) 'Establishing a sexual identity – case studies of learners with autism and learning difficulties.' *Autism, 13*, 551–566.

Warin, J. (2000) 'The attainment of self-consistency through gender in young children.' *Sex Roles, 42*, 209–232.

Zucker, K.J. and Bradley, S.J. (2000) 'Gender identity disorder.' In C.H. Zeanah (ed.) *Handbook of Infant Mental Health*, 2nd edn. New York: The Guildford Press.

Recommended reading

Attwood, S. (2008) *Making Sense of Sex.* London: Jessica Kingsley Publishers.

Crissey, P. (2004) *Personal Hygiene.* London: Jessica Kingsley Publishers.

Henault, I. (2005) *Asperger's Syndrome and Sexuality.* London: Jessica Kingsley Publishers.